ANIMAL ODYSSEYS

HIGH IN THE WIND: THE SNOW GEESE

Lynn M. Stone

THE ROURKE CORPORATION, INC.

Vero Beach, FL 32964

Photo Credits:

© Lynn M. Stone: all photos except pages as noted.
© Tom and Pat Leeson: cover, 8, 10, 45.

© 1991 The Rourke Corporation, Inc.

Library of Congress Cataloging in Publication Data

Stone, Lynn M.
    High in the wind: the snow geese / by Lynn M. Stone
      p. cm. – (Animal odysseys)
    Includes index.
    Summary: Describes the various "mysteries" about the snow goose's nature and habits which have been solved by scientific research.
    ISBN 0-86593-104-6
    1. Snow goose – Juvenile literature. [1. Snow goose. 2. Geese.] I. Title. II. Series: Stone, Lynn M. Animal odysseys.
QL696.A52S77 1991
598.4'1–dc20

                    90-40269
                      CIP
                      AC

ANIMAL ODYSSEYS

CONTENTS

1
BIRDS FROM BEYOND THE NORTH WIND

For many years the scientific name of the snow goose, *Anser hyperboreus*, fit it perfectly – like a down vest. The name meant "goose from beyond the north wind" and was well suited to the secretive, far-flying snow goose. Sky watchers in southern Canada and the United States knew that these big, white birds showed up every fall in flocks of thousands and that each spring they climbed into a cold sky and wheeled northward. But their northern home was a mystery. Where did the birds' northward **migration** take them each spring?

Ornithologists, the scientists who study birds, knew that snow geese must breed somewhere in the remote north, the arctic country, but until early in the twentieth century they were not sure where. Finally, after a great deal of searching and talking with native people in the north, ornithologists began to pinpoint the snow goose nesting grounds on the grassy arctic plains

Right:
The arctic nesting grounds of snow geese weren't known to scientists until the early twentieth century.

of northern Canada. Much more recently, in the early 1960s, another snow goose mystery was solved.

Ornithologists had long been puzzled by the true identity of some dark geese that nested in a few of the snow goose **colonies**. Called blue geese, they were a dusky-blue color with white heads. They were the same size as the snow geese, and they had the same habits and calls.

Early American ornithologists thought the blue geese were young snow geese. Later ornithologists assumed that they were a separate **species**, or kind, of goose. Finally, after studying blue geese and snow geese together in the Arctic for 30 years, ornithologists realized that the two species were actually one. The "blue" geese were just a color variation, or **phase**, of the all-white snow geese. Just as red foxes may be black and black

bears may be honey-colored, the geese, in some colonies, were both white and a bluish color. The observers in the Arctic found that white-phase snow geese sometimes mated with blue-phase birds. Some of their young were white and others were blue. Part of the reason that ornithologists were fooled for so long was that the nesting colonies of the blue-phase snow geese were not found until 1929.

Not all of the snow goose colonies have blue-phase birds. The number of blue geese in the colonies increases from west to east. The westernmost snow goose colonies have no blue-phase birds at all, but in some of the

Above:
"Blue" snow geese are a color phase.

colonies on Baffin Island, high in the Arctic, up to eighty percent of the geese are blue. Until ornithologists found the two color phases together, it had been quite easy to assume that each was a separate species.

With the discovery that blue geese and snow geese were one and the same, ornithologists found themselves with an extra scientific name. They had called the blue geese *Anser caerulescens*, "bluish goose." Since the blue goose had been named first, in the mid-1700s, its scientific name was kept and *hyperboreus* was discarded. Today all of the snow geese – whites and blues alike – are *caerulescens* to scientists. Their scientific name may not be as appealing as *hyperboreus*, but they are still the geese flying from beyond the north wind. Few people ever see snow geese on their arctic nesting grounds. Their summer retreats remain beyond the reach of roads, rails, and large aircraft.

During the remainder of the year, when they are migrating or at winter quarters, snow geese are much better known. South of the Arctic, snow geese thrill thousands of bird-watchers, **naturalists**, and **waterfowl** hunters, those who hunts ducks, geese, and swans. A flock of sunstruck snow geese gleaming in a blue sky is one of the great spectacles of North American wildlife. Watching snow geese sharply tilt and tumble earthward with a loud rush of air as they slip from side to side in rapid flight is even more impressive.

Snow geese create a stir wherever they go. They are impossible to ignore. Both color phases are striking, but the birds' constant chatter demands attention, too. Snow geese are probably the most talkative waterfowl on Earth. Their high-pitched yelps and cries can be deafening at close range. They can also be lyrical as they drift on the wind over **tundra**, **prairies**, rivers, and marshes. Perhaps nothing signals the passing seasons with finer tunes than the gentle, stirring music of snow geese.

To an untrained ear, the cries of snow geese sound like the cries of any wild geese. It is much easier to identify a snow goose by its appearance. The white-phase bird's body is entirely white except for its black wing tips and orange-pink beak, legs, and feet. The rusty-colored feathers on the bird's head are the result of feeding in water with a high iron content.

Blue-phase snow geese are quite distinct, too. Their heads and necks are white and their bodies blue-gray. Some have more white **plumage**, or feathering, than others. All snow geese have a "grinning patch." Their bill and its cutting edges close in such a way that the geese seem to have a fixed grinning expression.

The grinning patch helps separate the snow goose from its pint-sized relative, the Ross' goose. These little arctic geese wear the same white plumage and black wing tips as white snow geese. However, they are considerably smaller and lack the black grinning patch on their bills. The Ross' goose bill is also shorter, stouter, and "lumpier" than a snow goose's. A typical Ross' goose

Right:
The snow goose has a "grinning patch" and iron-stained plumage.

measures about 23 inches long. Snows measure from 25 to 38 inches.

Ross' geese and snow geese are similar enough to sometimes mate and produce young that have features of both parents. Even more alike are the two groups of snow geese. The smaller snow geese are often referred to as "lesser" snow geese. A population of larger snow geese, known as "greater" snow geese, nests in the arctic north of the lesser snow goose colonies. None of the greater snow goose colonies has any blue-phase birds. On the wintering grounds, the two **races** – a name given to slightly different members of the same kind – stay largely apart. The entire greater snow goose population winters on the east coast of the United States. Almost the entire lesser snow goose population winters on the west coast and along the Gulf of Mexico.

2
WINTER RESORTS

In the early 1920s ornithologist Arthur Cleveland Bent wondered how the blue goose, "such a large . . . species, which is numerically so abundant, can disappear so completely during the breeding season." Then, as now, there was nothing secret about the winter range of snow geese.

Nearly all of the blue-phase snow geese spend the winter months on the Gulf of Mexico coast between Vermillion Bay, Louisiana, and Galveston Bay, Texas. The white birds are more widespread. Huge flocks winter from the Louisiana border west along the gulf coast of Texas and south into Mexico. The entire population of greater snow geese – some 285,000 birds – winters along the mid-Atlantic coast from New Jersey south to North Carolina. Some of their haunts are long, broad saltwater inlets called **sounds**. Two favorites of the snow geese are the Currituck and Pamlico sounds of North Carolina. Other large flocks settle onto Chesapeake Bay, Back Bay, and Delaware Bay.

Left:

Snow geese and Canada geese pick corn kernels from a stubble field.

West of the Rocky Mountains, the largest number of snow geese – upward of 400,000 – winter in California's Central Valley. Other flocks, much smaller in size, winter along Puget Sound, Washington; in the Imperial Valley, California; at Bosque del Apache National Wildlife Refuge, New Mexico; and in scattered flocks elsewhere in California, Nevada, and Mexico.

Along the sea coasts, snow geese feed on such natural foods as bulrushes, widgeon grass, and spike rushes. Snow geese are "grubbers." They love to poke their bills into mud flats during low tides and probe for roots and stems. Wintering snow geese also feed in freshwater marshes and on agricultural land. Scattered rice, grass, growing cereal crops, and waste grains are a major part of the winter diet for many snow geese.

During the night, snow geese typically rest, or roost, on water. They make early daylight flights to a marsh or field. They spend much of the day feeding. They also rest and clean their feathers with their bills, an activity called **preening**. On moonlit nights they may extend their feeding activities.

Winter is a less demanding period for snow geese than other times of the year. They have neither the long, taxing flights of migration nor the pressure of nesting and raising young in the short arctic summer. But winter is not all relaxation. For young geese in their second winter, December means the start of courtship. Snow geese don't usually breed until their third winter, but they begin to choose mates during their second winter. The courtship involves displays both in the air and on the water. This activity, which may last from December into the spring, creates partnerships that sometimes last for life.

While the one-and-a-half year olds are searching for mates, the youngest birds are undergoing changes in their plumage. The light gray plumage of the juvenile white-phase geese is replaced by adult white. The uniform brownish-gray plumage of the dark geese is traded for the adult plumage of blue-phase geese.

Much of the snow goose's winter range is owned or managed by the United States Fish and Wildlife Service, part of the federal government. The Fish and Wildlife Service's network of national wildlife refuges, a system begun in the early 1900s, provides the geese with protection on their **traditional** wintering resorts. In addition, many of the refuges are managed for the welfare of geese. Refuge workers plant food crops for geese and manipulate water levels for their advantage. Some of the important winter refuges for snow geese are Pea Island, North Carolina; Anahuac, Texas; Lacassine, Louisiana; and the Sacramento National Wildlife Refuge, California.

3
TRAVELERS

Much of the mystery and fascination which we experience with wild geese evolves from their seasonal migrations. Like freight trains disappearing down distant tracks, the flocks of geese pass loudly by, then vanish. Only they know for sure where they have been and where they are going.

Below:
Migrations are rarely in neat V formations like this one.

Why the geese make these seasonal **odysseys** from one location to another is much easier to understand than how they make them. There are many good reasons for birds to migrate. One of the most obvious reasons is weather. The Arctic turns unbearably cold and harsh after the short northern summer. By migrating, the geese avoid the cold, but more importantly they avoid starvation. The arctic summer produces a feast of plants and insects for snow geese. The abundance of food is a plus; it makes the long journey north worthwhile. When autumn arrives, however, the food supply withers and dies. By migrating to the wetlands of the United States, far south of their **breeding range**, the snow geese find a rich and steady source of food. Migration puts the geese back into ideal feeding conditions.

The migration each fall from the Far North to the south makes sense. It is not as clear why the geese would want to leave the mild weather of their winter homes in the spring. Why not stay and avoid a long, difficult flight? For one thing, the cool climate of the north is probably more comfortable to the geese than the summer climate of the United States. The arctic climate may even be necessary for the development of young geese in ways not known to us.

There are certainly advantages to migrating north to the arctic plains. Geese benefit from a variety of foods, and nesting in the Arctic changes their diet considerably from the wintering sites. Space is another advantage, as

Above:

Snow goose goslings thrive in the cool climate of arctic summers.

is the type of vegetation in the north, which enables them to build thousands of nests on the ground away from people and most predators. The wintering grounds of snow geese would not be well-suited to their nesting style.

One reason geese travel north each spring may simply be because they always have. Flying north in the spring is a goose tradition. A tradition is something that has been done for generations on a regular schedule. For thousands of years snow geese have been migrating between the Arctic and the warm lands to the south. Unthinkingly, they continue to carry on the tradition.

17

Although there are advantages to migration, these flights from one abundant food source to another are not without a price. Perhaps the biggest cost for a migrating goose is the loss of energy. Migration is a grueling experience.

Geese and other waterfowl (ducks and swans) on migration fly on generally north-south routes that ornithologists call **flyways**. The Pacific flyway, for example, includes the nesting areas in the Pacific region, the flight routes west of the Rocky Mountains, and the wintering sites on and near the Pacific coast. Some of these Pacific flyway snow geese make a 4,000-mile flight from Wrangel Island, Siberia, to southern California. They don't make that journey non-stop, but it is nonetheless a difficult trip. Many of the youngest birds die of exhaustion along the way, especially in rough weather.

The real puzzle in migration studies is how snow geese find their way from the southern United States to a piece of barren ground in arctic Canada. That they do find their way, and that they have **homing ability**, is clear. But how they exercise this ability to find their traditional homes is not. Ornithologists certainly cannot quiz the geese. The scientists' best guess is that the geese may find their route by several means.

Apparently, geese can direct themselves in part by using the sun and, at night, the position of the stars as reference. Sailors on the oceans used the heavenly bod-

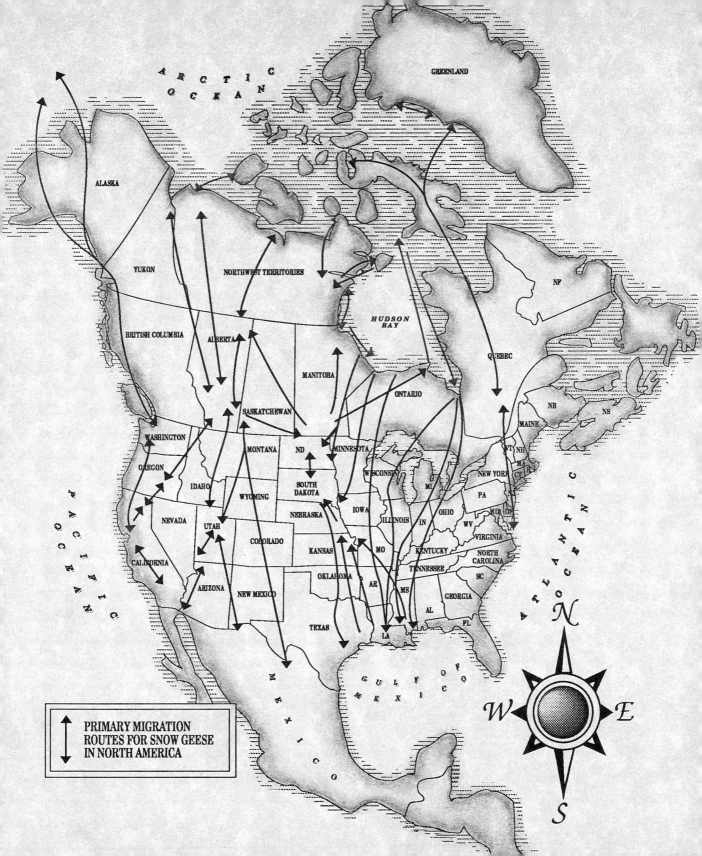

Left:
Snow geese find their way each spring to the distant arctic tundra.

ies in a similar way for centuries. Being tuned into the sun and stars, however, doesn't mean that snow geese ignore the Earth below them. They undoubtedly are conscious of shores, waterways, islands, and other important features of the land.

Somehow they learn migration routes and remember them. It is likely that young geese learn the route from their elders. The amazing element in migration is that the geese can recall enough to accurately reconstruct a journey that sometimes stretches 4,000 miles. (One of the snow goose's arctic neighbors, the golden plover, travels to South America, a distance of 8,000 miles.)

Snow geese and most of their goose cousins are born to migrate. Their lives are arranged around that fact. Just what triggers the actual migratory flight itself is not totally understood. Just before migrating north in

Right:
The golden plover nests on the tundra, then migrates 8,000 miles to South America.

the spring, geese become increasingly restless. They are unusually plump and they probably have excess energy. In addition, they are affected by the beginnings of the urge to nest. The warming temperatures, the lengthening periods of sunlight, and the behavior of other geese also contribute to their readiness for migration. Suddenly, one day when the weather is to their liking, they lift off and steer north. For snow geese, "good" weather means fairly clear skies and a moderate tail wind – a wind pushing them forward.

Does an old gander lead the flock? Do geese take turns being leaders? Neither question has been answered with certainty. Some flocks don't seem to have a leader. In a V formation one bird is clearly on the point, but geese are not always in V formations. They often fly in broad lines, in formations that resemble a barbless hook – J – and in no formation at all.

We know more about how high and how fast they fly than which goose leads the flock. In fact, snow geese fly at many different heights, or **altitudes**. They need to fly at least high enough to avoid objects on the landscape and rough air. Generally, wild geese in North America seem to fly between 750 and 3,500 feet. Weather conditions can force them to fly higher or lower. Snow geese have been recorded at altitudes up to 20,000 feet – nearly four miles up. But that is not typical, any more than are the 11,000-foot altitudes that some flocks reach to cross the Rocky Mountains.

The normal flying speed of migratory snow geese is between 25 and 37 miles per hour. They can fly faster than that over short distances. A brisk tail wind increases their speed, and head winds slow them.

4
HIGH IN THE SPRING WIND

The arctic pastures beckon the snow geese in late February and early March. The Arctic is far from ready for the geese; it is still locked in snow and ice. But the geese nevertheless feel the need to begin their northward trek. Once the journey begins, it will take most flocks 10 or 11 weeks to fly from their winter home to the Arctic.

Right:
The arctic has begun to thaw when the geese arrive in May.

The geese don't fly part of the distance each day. They make the trip in long flights sandwiched around a few days or weeks at a stop-over. At various gathering places along the northward routes, flocks that wintered at different sites come together. As spring advances northward, leaving a wet, muddy thaw in its wake, so do the snow geese.

The geese fly by day and moonlit night. They see more of America as they follow the retiring winter north than most people see in their lifetimes. Honking loudly, the flocks pass over prairies, marshes, wide rivers, snow-streaked fields, and muddy stubble. Some climb high into the sky and look down at mountain peaks. All of them fly over villages, highways, and the twinkling red lights of nighttime railroad crossings. Somehow, by watching this grand quilt of human and natural handi-work spread below them, they stay on course.

By mid-May, the flocks are poised for the final legs of their journeys. When in loud commotion the snow geese leave the northern prairies, they are Arctic-bound. Within 48 hours after the first flock's departure, all of the snow geese in the northern prairies have migrated north. They fly non-stop for at least 500 miles, passing above the great evergreen forest which lies like a broad, dark belt between prairie and tundra across mid-Canada. The evergreen forest is broken up by countless lakes, but they are poor in goose food and uninviting.

Not all of the snow geese are flying to the same destination. Some of the prairie flocks go no farther north than their nesting sites on the tundra's southern fringes. Others barrel onward to more northern nest sites high in the Arctic.

Westward of these flocks, which were gathered from central and Mississippi flyways, are the Pacific flyway geese. Their destinations are the nesting grounds of Wrangel Island, northern Alaska and the western Canadian Arctic.

The greater snow geese on the Atlantic flyway gather first at Delaware Bay. Then they make a direct flight to Cap Tourmente on the St. Lawrence River near Quebec. There are salt marshes to be grubbed and farm stubble to be picked. They stay in the vicinity of Cap Tourmente for most of April and early May. By then, the land of the little flowers, the land that called them in the first place, is preparing for their arrival.

5 LAND OF LITTLE FLOWERS

The summer home of the snow geese is the arctic tundra, one of the world's last great wildernesses. The tundra is the prairie of the Far North, a vast, spongy meadow of mosses, lichens, grasses, and tiny flowers. The tundra sweeps around the land regions of the Far North like a wide collar, stretching around the Canadian Arctic, northern Alaska, Siberia, and part of Greenland. In places it is a flat plain relieved only by boulders, gravel ridges, and scattered lumps of earth pushed upward by frost heaves. In other places, the tundra rolls upward onto the sides of hills and bleak mountains.

This is harsh, remote country. Because it is so far north, the ground only thaws a few inches even in the summer. Plants struggle for survival in such conditions, and trees, as we know them, are unknown. The little willow and birch trees of the tundra are no more than low, spreading shrubs trimmed and twisted by the wind.

Snow and ice, wind and unbelievable cold rule the tundra for eight months of the year. Very few animals

Above:
The tundra is a spongy mat of mosses, lichens, and little flowers.

can live year-round in these conditions. But when winter begins to loosen its wolflike grip in May, the tundra is transformed as if by magic into a wonderland of life. Rushing streams nibble away the ice. The lengthening days of sunshine thaw the tundra surface with amazing consequences. Pools and shallow lakes form everywhere. Rainfall and snowfall are light in the Far North, but because the air is dry and the ground is permanently frozen under the surface, the snow melt and rainfall neither evaporate nor drain. From the air, the tundra looks like an unending pasture of puddles, enormously appealing to ground-nesting water birds.

The geese – Canadas, white-fronts, snows, Ross' – begin to touch down in a hail of windblown calls at colonies across the Arctic. They are joined by ducks, tundra swans, loons, sandhill cranes, gulls, jaegers, and knots of shorebirds. If the tundra in late May is still napping, the chorus of birds and the crackle of ice will soon awaken it.

Below:
From the air the tundra looks like a pasture of puddles.

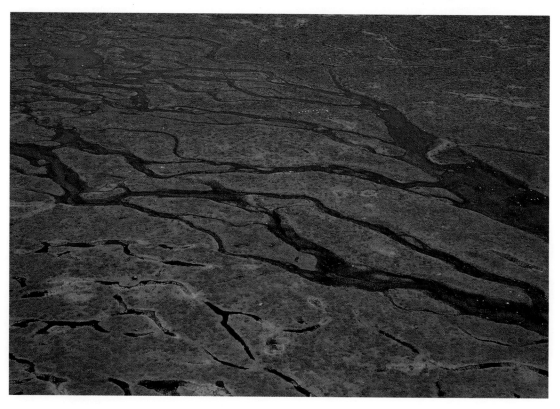

Above
At midnight in early July, a sunset fires up over a tundra lake.

Snow geese flock to a few traditional sites along arctic sea coasts, almost always near a river. The westernmost colony is in Russia, on Wrangel Island. Another 20 or so major colonies, each with at least 1,000 nests, are located eastward across the Arctic from northern Alaska to Baffin Island, Canada, and Greenland. The southernmost colony is at Cape Henrietta Maria on the shore of James Bay, an arm of Hudson Bay.

The timing of arrival is near-perfect in "normal" summers. With the onset of the arctic summer, the long days nourish new plants and an explosion of insects and other tiny animals. The birds have an immense nesting ground and a food source that grows richer each day.

Here, near the top of the world, the tundra in late June never lies in total darkness. The Earth's angle to the sun is such that daylight prospers, and the Arctic becomes the legendary "land of the midnight sun." Warmed and awakened, the tundra greens and releases the **nutrients** that are the base for the whole tundra community of plants and animals.

Caribou, the antlered nomads of the Far North, quickly splash across rocky streams. Loons wail on tundra lakes. Wolves dig out dens on the sides of gravel hills. Sandhill cranes tattoo the sky with their bugling cries. Tundra swans bob like white corks on a choppy stream where cold, silver-black grayling, slick as the river stones, rise for flies. The surge of life is an all-day celebration every day, but the animals know that the arctic summer is as fleeting as the caribou. A sense of urgency spurs them on with their purposes – to produce more of their kind and prepare for winter. In just three months the bird music of the summer tundra will be blown away by the howl of the north wind.

6 ARCTIC GOSLINGS

Snow geese waste no time settling into their nesting activities. On the tundra, there is no time to waste. The geese will have no more than 15 weeks to nest and raise their goslings to flying age. If the spring thaw is late and autumn is early, the geese have only 12 weeks in which to successfully raise their young.

When they arrive in the Arctic, the adult geese already have their mates. They don't have to take precious time to sort out who is going with whom. They immediately look for nest sites. Usually enough snow has melted so that slight rises in the tundra surface are available for snow-free nesting. Male geese, or ganders, choose a nest site and defend it if other ganders try to take it. The nest and the ground immediately around it become the pair's **territory**. Unlike the neighboring sandhill cranes, which require huge territories, snow geese stake out a small claim. In some snow goose colonies, as many as 1,000 pairs nest in each square mile.

The female goose builds the nest, a circle of grass, moss, and down from her breast. She often anchors the nest by building it next to a rock or in the outer branches of ankle-high willow or birch.

The goose lays from three to seven white eggs. The earliest nesting geese usually lay the most eggs. She doesn't immediately sit on her eggs for long periods of time. However, after the entire group of eggs – the **clutch** – has been laid, she begins staying on the nest, **incubating** the eggs to keep them warm.

Below:
A female snow goose incubates eggs that have begun to hatch.

Above:

A snow goose gander vigorously defends his nesting territory.

While the female incubates, she rarely leaves the nest for food and water. When she does leave, she plucks down from the nest rim and covers the eggs. By the end of the 23-day incubation period, her weight has dropped from about five pounds to four. Occasionally a goose becomes so weak that she finds herself unable to leave the nest, and she dies of starvation on her clutch of eggs.

The gander does not help incubate even if something happens to his mate. But he does stay near the nest, always guarding against **predators** like gulls and arctic foxes. Some ganders will challenge any intruder near the nest, even people. The gander's constant alert-

33

ness disrupts his eating habits, too, and he also loses weight during the incubation period.

Snow geese, especially the white birds, are easy to see on the tundra. Most tundra-nesting birds rely on their plumage blending with the yellow and brown colors of the tundra. That **camouflage** provides them with hiding and safety. Snow geese depend on their colonies and the aggressiveness of the ganders for safety. The hundreds or thousands of geese that compose a colony quickly alert each other to the presence of a predator.

On or about the twenty-third day of incubation, the eggs begin to crack. Each gosling inside an egg has a temporary "tooth" on its bill. The gosling uses it to chip away at the eggshell and eventually cracks it open.

Right:
Goslings quickly dry into bright-eyed fluffy balls of down.

Left:
These newly-hatched blue-phase snow goose goslings are wet and slippery.

34

Goslings hatch at nearly the same time. They are wet and slimy at birth, but the downy nest and the female's breast feathers, under which they huddle, help them dry quickly into fluffy balls of down. Within six to 24 hours after hatching, the youngsters are led away from the nest by the adult geese.

The female will shelter the goslings under her wings and breast whenever necessary for about two weeks. Otherwise, the little geese are independent. They feed themselves immediately. Mosquitoes are plentiful,

Above:
Snow geese lead their goslings away from the nest soon after they hatch.

and they are favorite **prey** of the goslings as they peck and tumble their way across the tundra.

Summer snowstorms can kill thousands of little geese during the first few days of life. After two or three weeks, however, the goslings have enough feathers and endurance to withstand freak storms.

In the long hours of daylight, baby snow geese grow quickly, partly because they feed 18 to 20 hours each day. By early September, at the age of two months, they weigh slightly over three pounds, more than 20 times the two-and-one-half ounces they weighed at birth.

For adult geese, no summer passes without a period of flightlessness. That is the time at which the geese undergo the **molt**, a change of feathers. The geese don't shed all their feathers, but they lose enough flight feathers to keep them earthbound for about 24 days. When the new feathers have grown in, the geese regain their ability to fly.

Usually the molt follows the hatch of the young. It is a difficult and dangerous time for the geese. They have unusual demands for energy because they are trying to replace lost weight and, at the same time, provide themselves with the energy needed for the growth of new feathers. They are also unable to fly from predators, although adult snow geese are rarely attacked.

7
PREDATORS AND PREY

In the tundra community of plants and animals, snow geese are among the plant eaters. As adults, they feed on tundra vegetation, such as grass, willow leaves, sedges, horsetail, mosses, and berries. They pluck these foods with their bills, using the cutting edges along the bill to grasp the plant. A hungry goose can make over 100 pecks in a minute.

Snow geese share the tundra with several other plant-eating animals. Some of them are the arctic ground squirrel, lemming, arctic hare, ptarmigan, caribou, and, on the northernmost tundra, musk ox. All of the plant eaters take their energy from the tundra plants and grow from eating them. The predators of the tundra live by eating the plant eaters. Energy is thus transferred from sunlight to plants, from plants to the plant-eating animals, and from the plant eaters to the meat eaters.

Each predator has preferred prey, although the choice of prey changes with the season. The little arctic fox is not big enough to dream of killing caribou, but it is

Above:

The arctic fox is white in winter, but it wears earth tones in the summer.

an enthusiastic hunter of birds until most of the birds fly south. Wolves, on the other hand, are large enough to kill any of the plant eaters, but they seem to prefer caribou. They rarely invade snow goose colonies.

Adult snow geese, in fact, are rarely killed by any animal. But snow goose eggs and goslings are frequently prey for foxes, gulls, and a gull-like bird called the jaeger. Unguarded nests and goslings that become sepa-

Left:
*The herring
gull often nests
near snow
goose colonies
and swipes
eggs and
goslings.*

rated from their parents are the most frequent targets. Although a female snow goose covers her eggs with down when she leaves the nest, a jaeger will pull the down away to see what is underneath. Sandhill cranes, too, occasionally prey on snow goose goslings and eggs.

During migration stopovers and at their winter homes, snow geese may be killed by coyotes, bald eagles, or great horned owls. Their only serious predator outside the Arctic, however, is man.

Snow geese are popular game for hunters in Canada and the United States each autumn. Eskimos and northern Indians still take a few geese on the nesting grounds, but the colonies are essentially under the protection of the Canadian government. Snow geese don't usually face gunfire until their autumn migration. Over 200,000 are shot in the United States alone each fall and early winter.

Each winter the U.S. Fish and Wildlife Service conducts flights to count snow geese. The totals rise and fall somewhat depending on the summer's nesting success, but the population of snow geese has been creeping upward in recent years. While the number of geese has grown, America's duck population has been tumbling.

In a given winter, there are approximately 2,500,000 snow geese in the United States. The population of greater snow geese has risen dramatically, from 35,000 in the winter of 1956-57 to nearly 300,000 in the late 1980s. Exactly why the snow goose population is increasing is not clear, but the Fish and Wildlife Service feels that the birds could now be hunted more intensely. To further that goal, the Fish and Wildlife Service may increase daily bag limits, the legal number of geese a hunter can kill in one day. The Fish and Wildlife Service does not always recognize the fact that far more people take pleasure from watching and listening to snow geese than from killing them.

Left:
The willow ptarmigan is one of the few birds that lives on the tundra all year.

8
HIGH IN THE AUTUMN WIND

By early September the tundra is tinted brown. The days are much shorter and the nights are chilled. The geese are fat and restless. They seem to know that there is no future on the tundra. Winter is always just a few inches away in the frozen soil. And now, it seems, winter is also riding a knife-sharp wind from the north.

The geese gather in loud flocks, testing their wings, flying, alighting, and flying up again. One day the urge to leave is overwhelming. With a chorus of goose talk and a flurry of wings, the flocks begin to climb high over the maze of ponds, islands, ridges, and river fingers that have been their home. Throughout the Arctic, wherever they have nested, the snow geese abandon their colonies in September. The snowy owls will remain with the ptarmigan and ravens. Somehow, along with the fox, weasel, and the wolf, they will eke out a living during the arctic winter. The shorebirds, gulls, numerous song-birds, cranes, loons, ducks, and swans retreat south-ward.

43

The northernmost nesting snow geese meet with more southern nesters at various gathering places, such as Cape Churchill, Manitoba, and James Bay, where hundreds of thousands of snows gather from mid-September to late October. They turn the southern shores of James Bay into an incredible army of geese. When the goose army departs, it is a spectacle. On a clear day, clouds of snow geese leave at once chased by a northern breeze. Some of the flocks leaving James Bay fly for nearly 60 hours without stopping, arriving during the third day on the coast of Louisiana. Meanwhile, in September and October, other flocks have reached the big prairie refuges at Sand Lake, South Dakota; DeSoto National Wildlife Refuge along the Iowa-Nebraska border; and Squaw Creek, Missouri. The western flocks have flown into the Puget Sound region of Washington and the Klamath wetlands along the California-Oregon border. During November and December the geese leave these midway sanctuaries and fly on to winter homes.

Below:
Clouds of snow geese leave the arctic colonies in September and migrate to the United States.

The greater snow geese arrive at Cap Tourmente in September. It is normally their only migration stop. They stay until November, when the ice and snow prod them onward to winter quarters along the mid-Atlantic coast.

By December the white and blue geese have settled into their winter homes. But it is a brief settlement. Soon the seasonal restlessness will haunt them again, and they will be on another journey to places beyond the north wind.

45

GLOSSARY

altitude – the height of an object above ground

breeding range – that portion of an animal's natural environment in which it produces young

camouflage – concealment by means of blending an animal's natural coloration with the environment

clutch – the eggs in a bird's nest

colony – a group of nesting animals of the same kind

flyway – a generally north-south flight path of migratory birds, including their summer and winter homes

homing ability – the ability to accurately return a considerable distance to a location, such as a birthplace

incubate – to keep eggs warm until they hatch

migration – a predictable seasonal movement from one location to another some distance away

molt – the loss of feathers

naturalist – a student of nature

nutrient – something that furnishes nourishment

odyssey – a long journey

ornithologist – a scientist who studies birds

phase – a particular color within a group of animals that produces two or more color types

plumage – the covering of feathers on a bird

prairie – the land of midwestern and western North America dominated by wild grasses and other non-woody plants; native grassland

predator – an animal that kills and feeds on other animals

preen – to carefully clean and oil feathers

prey – an animal hunted for food by another animal

race – slightly different groups within the same larger group, such as *greater* and *lesser* snow geese

species – a group of plants or animals whose members reproduce naturally only with other plants or animals of the same group; a particular kind of plant or animal, such as a *snow* goose

sound – a long, broad inlet of the ocean

territory – a home area defended by certain animals that live within it

traditional – that which has been done for generations and has been passed on from one generation to the next

tundra – the treeless mat of grasses, mosses, and lichens in the Far North above the evergreen forests

waterfowl – ducks, geese, and swans

INDEX

Numbers in boldface type refer to photo and illustration pages.

Snow geese often fly long distances non-stop, but they have favorite resting sites. During their spring and fall migrations, the geese can be seen easily if you know where these stopovers are and when the geese are likely to be there. On autumn flights south from the Arctic, snow geese begin to reach stopovers in September and early October. The greater snow geese, for example, usually gather in the largest numbers at Cap Tourmente, Quebec, between October 5-10. The leading flocks of the spring migration north begin their first northern stopovers in late February and March.

Winter is an excellent time to find snow geese at predictable locations. Huge concentrations of these birds can be seen at several national wildlife refuges and on some state conservation areas as well. It is always a good idea, however, to call ahead and ask wildlife rangers about the birds' precise whereabouts.

Snow Goose Migration and Wintering Sites

Anahuac National Wildlife Refuge, Anahuac, TX

Blackwater National Wildlife Refuge, Cambridge, MD

Bombay Hook National Wildlife Refuge, Smyrna, DE

Cap Tourmente, 30 miles east of Quebec City, Quebec

DeSoto National Wildlife Refuge, Missouri Valley, IA

Lacassine National Wildlife Refuge, Lake Arthur, LA

Pea Island National Wildlife Refuge, Manteo, NC

Sabine National Wildlife Refuge, Sulphur, LA

Sacramento National Wildlife Refuge, Willows, CA

Sand Lake National Wildlife Refuge, Columbia, SD

Squaw Creek National Wildlife Refuge, Mound City, MO

Ed. Note: Sites listed here do not represent *all* the places used by migrating and wintering snow geese. They do represent sites that are reliable and have relatively easy access.